E. H Dodge

Mount Desert Island, and the Cranberry Isles

E. H Dodge

Mount Desert Island, and the Cranberry Isles

ISBN/EAN: 9783743321694

Manufactured in Europe, USA, Canada, Australia, Japa

Cover: Foto ©ninafisch / pixelio.de

Manufactured and distributed by brebook publishing software
(www.brebook.com)

E. H Dodge

Mount Desert Island, and the Cranberry Isles

Mount Desert

ISLAND,

AND THE

Cranberry Isles.

"A noted Isle,
with lofty mountains, a rocky soil."

ELLSWORTH·
N. K. Sawyer, Printer.
1871.

INDEX.

Mt. Desert Island and the Cranberry Isles.

MT. DESERT ISLAND.

A millennium ago only the underpinning of Mt. Desert was formed, and this, to uphold the stagnant current, or divide the sweeping glaciers.

"Wonderful it is, that out of the bald, barren rock, life should spring; that over its surface a generous soil should spread, bearing its wealth of flowers, and fruits, and grains; giving 'seed to the sower, and bread to the eater.'"

Passing from a sunken ledge to an island field of plenty — from bleakness to beauty — from death to life is marvelous, yet we trace the steady transition.

The work of Dr. Seely explains the change:—Under atmospheric influences a trifle of the surface rock crumbled and dissolved. The lichen, the humble but efficient pioneer of vegetation and of life, fixed itself upon the decaying rock and found a home. The first was but a signal of a troop, and they came till the rock was grey with their patchwork. Dying, they mingled their decaying mass with the disintegrating rock. On the thin film of soil thus prepared another low, yet higher form of vegetation, the moss, appeared, and the grim rock grew grey with verdant life. Under the shade of this humid covering, the degradation of the rock hastened, and with the crumbled mass a greater mass of dying vegetation blended. The grass came next, and carpeted the whole with green; lived and died, and dying yielded its contribution to the soil. Then the low shrub found a foothold, and embossed work made the carpet more beautiful. Low trees soon mingled with the shrubs, and finally larger ones, the glory of the mountain, made the former waste a dwelling-place of beauty. The soil that bore all these is now rich,—rich, because death and air have made it the garden of life. Down to the deepest depth of the mold, down to

the granite rock, the soil was made rich by the mingling of that which
was once verdant with life. Lichen, and moss, and shrub, and tree,
have given their bodies that the race following might be more luxuri-
ous by their life and death. As over the buried cities of Herculaneum,
Pompeii and Strabea, new life ebbs and flows, so over the dead vegetation the fields grow green and golden in turn—so the wall of coral
rock converted itself into the "Island of Mt. Desert."

SITUATION AND CONNECTION OF THE ISLAND.

Mt. Desert Island is situated on the eastern coast of Maine, in Lat.
44 deg. 15 min. North, and Long. 68 deg. 20 sec. from Greenwich, West,
and from Washington, 8 deg. 40 min. East. It is about 150 miles from
Portland by Coast Pilot, and nearly 100 miles by the same reckoning
from the mouth of the St. Croix River, or what is called the " Lines."
It is connected to the mainland by a toll bridge over the Narrows of
Jordan's River. The mail communications are by stage, three times
per week, and by steamboat two. A telegraph line is established and
in operation from South West Harbor via Somesville to Ellsworth, and
one connecting Bar Harbor and Somesville.

Travelers' Guide, 1871. The stages are conducted by the proprietors,
Messrs. John and Eben Harden of Trenton, gentlemen in every sense
of the word, polite and agreeable to passengers and accommodating
to patrons. Their time table is as follows:—Leave Ellsworth every
Tuesday, Thursday and Saturday at 8 o'clock, A. M., arriving at the
termini at 2 o'clock, P. M. Returning—leave South West Harbor at 6
o'clock, A. M., arriving at Ellsworth at 12 M. By the mail arrange-
ments which began the 1st of July, 1871, there is a divide at the Mt.
Desert Post Office; the main stage goes direct to South West Harbor,
and the branch stage round the western side of the town with the Seal
Cove and (Bass Harbor) Tremont mails. The Bar Harbor or East
Eden Post Office stage branches off at the Narrows and goes down the
Eden road. There is a daily mail stage from Ellsworth to East Eden
Post Office, Bar Harbor, in the summer, from July 1st to October 1st.

The "Telegraph Line" between Ellsworth and Tremont (office at
the Island House, S. W. Harbor) was completed in July, 1870, through
the vigorous effort of Henry Clark, Esq., President of the Ellsworth

and Tremont Telegraph Company. The following is the first dispatch sent over the Bar Harbor and Mt. Desert line.

" EDEN, May 19, 1871.

From the Mayor of Eden to the Mayor of Bangor:

Eden sends a telegraphic greeting to Bangor. Our line will be completed by Eve; but owing to the rocky soil, not without A—dam."

The operators are, South West Harbor, Miss Abbie May Holden; Somesville, Mr. Roscoe G. Salsbury; Bar Harbor, Miss Reynolds.

The Steamer Lewiston, Capt. Deering, leaves Railroad Wharf, Portland, for Machiasport, every Tuesday and Friday evenings, at 10 o'clock, or on arrival of the 6 o'clock P. M. Steamboat Express train from Boston, touching at Rockland, Castine, Deer Isle, Sedgwick, Mt. Desert, Milbridge and Jonesport. Returning, leaves Machiasport every Monday and Thursday morning at 5 o'clock, touching at the afore named places, arriving in Portland in ample time for passengers to take the early morning train for Boston. Through tickets for sale by the early trains at the offices of the Boston and Maine, and Eastern Railroads.

The Lewiston touches at Bar Harbor (Mt. Desert) each trip from the 30th of June to the 15th of September, in addition to her landings at South West Harbor.

TIME TABLE.

Going East Leaves		Going West Leaves	
Boston at	6:00 P. M.	Machiasport at	5:00 A. M.
Portland	10:00 "	Jonesport,	6:30 "
Rockland,	5:00 A. M.	Millbridge,	8:00 "
Castine,	7:00 "	Mt. Desert,	11:00 "
Deer Isle,	8:00 "	Sedgwick,	1:00 P. M.
Sedgwick,	8:30 "	Deer Isle,	1:30 "
Mt. Desert,	11:30 "	Castine,	3:00 "
Millbridge,	3:00 P. M.	Rockland,	5:30 "
Jonesport,	4:30 "	Arrive at Portland at	12:00 Midnight.
Arriving at Machiasport at	6:00 "	" " Boston at	10:30 A. M.

State rooms and through tickets can be secured at No. 82 Washington Street, Boston. J. W. Richardson, Agent, Boston, and Ross and Sturdivant, Agents, Portland. The accommodations on board the Lewiston are superior,—officers worthy and affable—attendants kind and generous.

The Steamer Argo, Capt. Kissam, leaves Ellsworth for Belfast every Monday, Wednesday and Friday, at 6 o'clock, A. M., touching Mt. Desert, at Hodgdon's Landing, Brooklin, Sedgwick, Deer Isle and Castine, arriving in Belfast in time to connect with Sanfords' Independent Line for Boston; also connecting with the Maine Central Railroad for Augusta, Portland and Boston. Returning—leaves Belfast for Ellsworth and the above-named landings every Tuesday, Thursday and Saturday morning, on arrival of the Steamers Cambridge and Katahdin. The steamer Argo is a good substantial side-wheel boat of 250 tons burthen, with good accommodations for passengers, and in first class order.

·

HISTORY OF MT. DESERT.

"The Bald Mountain's shrubless brow—
The gray and thunder smitten Pile
Which marks afar the Desert Isle,"

Was first seen by John Cabot, the Venetian, though an inhabitant of Bristol. England, who received a commission from Henry VII., and sailed in the beginning of May, 1497, on a voyage of discovery, accompanied by his son. Sebastian Cabot; and one or both of them discovered the continent of North America, the year before the main land of South America had been discovered by Columbus, and two years before it had been discovered by Americus.

Worcester's History, page 257, 18 v., says: "The land first seen was called Prima Vista, which is supposed to have been a part of Newfoundland. They proceeded further north, in search of a passage to India, but finding no appearance of one, they tacked about and sailed as far as Florida. They erected crosses along the coast, and took a formal possession of the country in behalf of the crown of England. This was the foundation of the English claim to North America."

In 1620, a patent was granted by King James, to the Duke of Lenox, Ferdinando Gorges, and others, styled, "The Council of Plymouth, in the County of Devon, for settling and governing New England." This patent granted to them the country extending from lat. 40 deg. to 48 deg. N.,—or. from Philadelphia to St. John, Newfoundland.

When Sir Walter Raleigh. with his twelve armed vessels, sailed for Guinea, to develop the immense gold mines, which he reported vaulted the island, the Spaniards and Portuguese who had settlements there, and were working a small mine at St. Thomas, resolved, through courage and avarice, to show themselves superior, not only in arts and arms, but also in justice of quarrel; they applied to Alexander, VI., who then filled the papal chair (1618); and he generously bestowed on the Spaniards the whole western, and on the Portuguese the whole eastern part of the globe.

In 1603, Henry IV, of France, granted to Sieur de Monts, all the country included between the fortieth and the forty-sixth degrees of latitude North, or, from Philadelphia to Quebec. Thus it seems that Mt. Desert was claimed, by different grants and considerations, long before it was settled.

It is reasonably supposed, that one of the land marks raised by John Cabot or his son Sebastian, was on Mt. Desert, or " Coaste Hilles," as reported, from which so many eastern vessels took their departure, bound further up or down the coast. Other claims besides these mentioned, have taken in about the same territory, indeed, it would be impossible to disentangle the different grants which embraced the same lattitude.

The Protestants, who acknowledged not the authority of the Roman Pontiff, established the first discovery as the foundation of their title; and if a pirate or sea adventurer of their nation had but erected a stick or stone on the coast, as a memorial of his taking posession, they concluded the whole continent belonged to them, and thought themselves entitled to expel or exterminate, as usurpers, the ancient possessors or inhabitants.

We begin the settlement of Mt. Desert with De Monts. An effort to inaugurate the settlements before this time would be fruitless, unless, by some mystic revelation, we could trace the pedigree of the lost tribe of Israel.

On the sixth of May, 1604, De Monts arrived, with his two vessels, at a harbor on the south-east coast of Acadie. Poutrincourt, his associate, was in command of one of the vessels, and Nicholas D'Aubri, a priest, accompanied them on their first voyage. They landed on the island to replenish their supply of water, and while the crew were filling the tanks and tubs, D'Aubri, who, with a party went to explore the forest and reconnoitre the lakes, stopped at one of the brooks to drink, and as he bent over the water his sword escaped from the scabbard; he did not miss it until he reached the boat, then went back to find it and lost his way; his companions made search, but were obliged to leave him to his fate; sixteen days he wandered round the shore, praying for deliverance from solitude, and the terror of such a death as seemed inevitable; he was at last rescued by a party of his own men, who had returned to the island in search of reputed gold and silver plate and money, and carried back to his companions who received him as one from the dead.

De Monts did not remain long at Acadie; trouble with the fishermen and the traders caused Henry to extinguish the patent.

Poutrincourt went to Port Royal (now Annapolis, N. S.) and sent Biencourt, his son, to France, in 1608, for a supply of men and provisions. Their application to the French Government for assistance seemed to awaken the attention of Catholicism to the new world. The

2

King made a condition of his aid to the enterprise, "that attempts should be made to convert the natives to the Catholic Faith. The Jesuits commissioned to the work were Fathers Biarde and Masse, who embarked with Biencourt. On their arrival, Poutrincourt returned to France, leaving his son in command of Port Royal. These priests assumed rather more authority in the temporal management of the settlement than was wholesome to Biencourt, who told them that it was his part to rule them on earth, and theirs to point out to him the road to Heaven. They threatened him with the anathemas of the Catholic church, and he threatened them with a pugilistic chastisement.

Somehow the priests found their way to Mt. Desert, the same year. Williamson's History locates the place as selected by the Missionaries, "on the western side of the pool," or Somes' Sound, just at Somesville. Whittier says

"Far up the river have come:
They have left their boats—they have entered the wood,
And filled the depth of solitude
With the sound of the rangers' drum.
The hermit priest who lingers now—
While gazing on the scene below,
May half forget the dream of home,
That nightly with his slumbers come,—
The tranquil skies of sunny France,
The peasant's harvest song and dance,
The vines around the hillside wreathing,
The soft airs midst their clusters breathing,
The wings which dipped, the stars which shone
Within thy bosom, blue Garonne!
And round the Abbey's shadowed wall,
At morning spring and even fall,
    Sweet voices in the still air singing,—
The chant of many a holy hymn,—
    The solemn bell of vespers ringing,—
And hallowed torch-light falling dim
On pictured saint and seraphim!
For here beneath him lies unrolled,
Bathed deep in morning's flood of gold,
A vision gorgeous as the dream
Of the beautified may seem,
When, as his Church's legends say,
Borne upward in ecstatic bliss,
The rapt enthusiast soars away
Unto a brighter world than this;
A mortal's glimpse beyond the pale,—
A moment's lifting of the veil!"

Here they formed and fortified a habitation, and entered with great zeal upon the work of converting the natives to Christianity. It is probable there were no inhabitants but the savages. After five years' labor, with little or no success, they returned to Port Royal.

In the meantime, Madame Gurcheville, a lady very near to Marie de Medicis, and famed for her beauty and piety, obtained a transfer of the grant of De Monts, to which Louis Fourteenth added all of North America from the 25th to the 50th degrees of latitudes, or, from Cape Florida to the St. Lawrence. By subscription, and through the influence of her friends at court, she fitted out a ship under the command of one Saussage, her agent, and accompanied by Du Thet, a priest, to plant the cross in the wilderness of Acadie.

The ship arrived at Port Royal in the spring of 1613; they found the settlement reduced to utter misery. Biarde and Masse, with three others, joined the ship's company, and they sailed for a more moderate latitude—westward. When off Mt. Desert, they experienced heavy weather,—storms and furious gales, with fog, drove them close to the stone-walled shore, so near, that in the calm which followed, the ship was thrown upon the head-land, by the old surge of the undertow and the incoming tide. They effected a landing, however, set up a cross, and in gratitude for their escape from the maddened elements, dedicated the spot "Saint Sauveur."

Biarde situated the place as three leagues from their first habitation on the pool. There is a difference among writers, who have attempted and assumed to show to the present people of Mt. Desert, the locality of St. Sauveur, but from the most reliable comparison, and positive reasoning, it is evident that it was somewhere between South West Harbor, lower dist., and East Bass Harbor; and the landing place at Ship Harbor, just to the east of Bass Harbor Head; local tradition makes it so—hence, the name—Ship Harbor. The oldest inhabitants say their earliest information was such. One responsible man says he was told by an old lady living in Warren, that her Grandmother was wrecked, when a little girl, at the precise spot mentioned; in the earlier moiety of the 19th century, and then after much suffering was carried to Virginia. This is given by no less a person than Colonel James Crockett of Rockland,—and as we listened to his story, we

> "We seem to look
> Upon the Jesuit's Cross and Brook,—
> On the brow of a hill, which slopes to meet
> The flowing tide, and bathe its feet,—
> The bare washed rock, and the drooping grass,
> And the creeping vine, as the waters·pass,—
> A rude and unshapely chapel stands,
> Built up in that wild by unskilled hands;
> Yet the traveller knows it a place of prayer,
> For the holy sign of the cross is there:
> And should he chance at that place to be,
> Of a Sabbath morn, or some hallowed day,
> When prayers are made, and masses are said,
> Some for the living and some for the dead,
> Well might that traveller start to see
> The tall dark forms, that take their way
> From the birch canoe, on the river shore,
> And the forest paths to the chapel door;
> And marvel to mark the naked knees
> And the dusky torcheads bending there,
> While, in coarse white vesture, over these
> In blessing or in prayer,
> Stretching abroad his thin pale hands,
> Like a shrouded ghost, the Jesuit stands."

It would occupy considerable space to give all the facts which make the theory true; so much, given on local logic, agrees perfectly with history. One thing more may be added, though,—the three leagues spoken of by Biarde. is equivalent to twelve French miles, about the distance from Somesville to Bass Harbor.

During their stay a fort was built, gardens planted, farming, fishing and hunting made up their avocation.

The different accounts are so conflicting as to the length of their sojourn, that no real time can be opinioned; they must have staid more than one season, though, because Madame de Gurcheville supplied them with their stores, ammunition and church furniture.

Capt. Samuel Argal, Governor of South Virginia, was cast away on one of his fishing voyages to the coast of Maine, a little further up the bay, somewhere near Castine. The natives told him about the Catholic reign at St. Sauveur, which fired his indignation and opened his angry veins. He returned home, raised an expedition to expel them as intruders upon the North and South Virginia patent. Eleven fishing vessels, sixty men, and fourteen pieces of small cannon comprised the force under Commodore Argal. The French were unprepared for an attack—many were away from the fort at the time; guns were dismounted, and only a feeble resistance made. The fleet fired only one broadside. Du Thet was killed and a few wounded. Argal took possession in the name of the King, and carried the larger part of the settlement, with Biarde, to Virginia. Masse, with a few others, escaped to the woods and manœuvered clear of the Englishmen, and through the influence of the English Ministry, was allowed to remain on the island sometime afterward.

> "Ah, weary priest!—with pale hands pressed
>   On thy throbbing brow of pain,
> Baffled in thy life long quest,
>   Overworn with toiling vain,
> How ill thy troubled musings fit
> The holy quiet of a breast
> With the Dove of Peace at rest,
> Sweetly brooding over it,
> Thoughts of strife, and hate, and wrong
> Swept thy heated brain along,—
> Hoary priest! thy dream is done
> Of a hundred red tribes won
> To the pale of the Holy Church."

The place of the action just described, was down by the sea-wall, and some relics of the old fort have been found in the present century.

Governor Winthrop, who sailed from Cowes, April 8, 1630, in the ship Lady Arabella, made land on the eighth day of June, and reported it in his journal as Mt. Mansel for the French.

Champlain first named the island "Monts Desert," in compliment to De Monts, and from its wild and bald appearance,—hence, the modern accent,—Mount Des-ert.

It is evident the red men inhabited the island, as relics of various sorts were not uncommon, even within a few years, but, since rusticators and itemizers have visited the island they have disappeared.

The island appears in history again in 1688, by M. la Motte Cadilliac, who received from Louis XIV., a grant containing one hundred thousand acres, embracing the whole neighborhood of Mt. Desert. He made a vigorous effort to maintain his grant, but was obliged to leave it in 1713, after the whole territory of Acadie had been ceded to England by the treaty of Utrecht. Cadilliac retained, with proud affection, the memory of his island dominion, and during the remainder of life, autographed himself " Lord of Mt. Desert."

All those old places are now

"Arched over by the ancient woods,
Which time, in those dull solitudes,
Wielded the dim axe of Decay,
Alone hath ever shorn away."

Up to 1761, the island was uninhabited, save by Indians, and the frequent visits of coasters, traders, fishermen and surveyors.

Suspending a few years, we take up the romantic history of the French again, in the persons of M. and M'me. de Gregoire. After the war of the revolution, the old French claim recognized to any part of our coast, was allowed by the General Court of Massachusetts. George Bernard, who formerly by a grant owned the whole island, lost his title by confiscation. His son, John Bernard of Bath, who had been a Whig during the war, had restored to him half of the island; the dividing line was,—South West Harbor, Somes' Sound—thence north-west to the shore on Jordan's River.

The following quotation is the most reliable, concerning the Gregoires we have been able to find. It was written by the Editor of the Republican *Journal*, in September, 1853 :

" In November, 1786, Mons. Gregoire claimed in right of his wife, by virtue of a grant made to her grandfather, M. la Motte Cardilliac. General Lafayette had written to M. Otto, French charge to our Government in favor of the claim, and it was granted from this consideration. M. Gregoire and those with him were naturalized by special act of Congress, and became possessors of public lands in Mt. Desert. Many of the land titles recorded in the Hancock Registry are from M. Gregoire. There are now on the island few if any of the descendants of the original French settlers."

De Costa says :
" Here, near Hull's Cove, dwelt Madame Marie Therese de Gregoire, a descendant of De la Motte Cardilliac. It appears that in the year 1688, the King of France gave to Cardilliac a large tract of land on the mainland, together with the Island of Mt. Desert, of which he took nominal possession, and executed several papers in which he styled himself ' Lord of Donaquee and Mt. Desert,' Donaquee was the Indian name for what is now Union River. M'me. Gregoire, in company with her husband, Barthelemy de Gregoire, appeared before the General Court of Massachusetts, sitting in Boston, petitioning for the confirmation of her right, as grand-daughter to Cardilliac. The Court heard and granted her plea, July, 6, 1787, and afterwards by a special act naturalized Madame, her husband and children, Pierre, Nicholas and Marie. Madame Gregoire came in possession of about 60,000 acres, embracing parts of the mainland and the entire island, except where already occupied by actual settlers."

It is probable they lacked the essential elements to succeed as pion-
eers, for in less than ten years they sold the most of their estate to
William Bingham. They died in 1810, and their graves, or the spot
where they were buried, is just outside of the graveyard, at Hull's
Cove. Protestantism, or liberal prejudice would not allow them to be
interred inside the cemetery walls,—at least, so runs the tradition, yet,
it was the same to them, as long as the place was not blessed by a
priest with book and cross; and there they are, if the reader can
imagine where, the last relics of the French on Mt. Desert.

It has been impossible for us to learn what ever became of Pierre,
Nicholas and Marie, but it is supposed they returned to France to
occupy an inherited estate. If either of them are living, it would seem
proper, and filial duty, to some way inhearse the remains of their
parents or perpetuate the memory of their resting place.

TOPOGRAPHY OF THE ISLAND.

The greatest length of the island is fifteen miles, in a line from Bass
Harbor headland to Sand Point, Eden; and the greatest width " from
shore to shore," is ten miles. It is twelve miles from Seal Cove, Tremont, to Bar Harbor, Eden, and fourteen miles trom Bass Harbor
head to the toll-bridge, as near as can be reckoned by the most accu-
rate survey that has yet been made. The whole island measures about
one hundred and thirty square miles, and is nearly equally divided,
reckoning the little islands, belonging to the several towns, Eden, Mt.
Desert and Tremont. The town lines run irregularly east and west,
portioning to Tremont the south and south-west peninsular land; to
Mt. Desert, an uneven latitudinal belt; and to Eden the whole northern end, in shape like the disarranged outlines of a hemi-cy-cle. The
shores are curiously wrought, with dangerous reefs and safe harbors;
—" many a bold projecting point is seen extending far, while harbors
intervene."

Where Somes' Sound leaves its waters in South West Harbor—the
shores form a nook like bay, with the Cranberry Isles moved out far
enough to form a breakwater. The principal harbors on the island

coast are North East Harbor, South West Harbor and Bass Harbor. The names North East and South West are attached to the harbor on account of their range from Greening's Island. Bass Harbor took its name from the fact that it was once filled with those kind of fish which inhabited the waters at the time of its first settlement, and a weir was built for taking them, across the entrance of Richardson's Cove on the eastern shore.

We name these as the principal harbors, because they are most frequented by vessels bound up or down the coast.

South West Harbor is the largest on the coast, and as safe as any, —it has an entrance—eastern and western.

Bar Harbor is on the North East coast of the island, and takes its name from the bar which connects it to one of the Porcupine Islands. It is a smooth harbor, always quiet, even in the turmoil of the gale.

The other harbors are all deep, and good holding-ground for anchorage. The harbors on the western coast are Goose Cove, Seal Cove, and Sawyer's Cove; each derived its name from the title-name it bears.

One fact concerning the superior privilege for boating, is, the waters flow gradually in the harbors, and there is no swift current in the surrounding bays,—boats sail out of the basin harbors, on the mimicking bays, and then farther on, the dark fringes of the ocean. The harbor landings are as smooth as lake shores, apparently without an ebb or flow, but down the mountain shore the under-current heaves up against the granite wall with terrible force, grand and awful.

There is such a contrast in the different characters of the island, that it is difficult to make an explicit topography—without the sight of a map, and the accompanying one, taken from the actual survey of every road and place, will better explain itself.

The mountains lie in a range, beginning one half mile from Seal Cove, Tremont, to Somes Sound, then they are scattered over the south eastern portion of the towns of Mt. Desert and Eden. Green Mountain, which is the third in range from the eastern shore, is 1,762 feet above the mean level of the sea, according to the U. S. Coast Survey, on which was the principal station. In front of Green Mountain "some huge nameless rocks are ascending." The mountains, are called by the inhabitants as they range from west to east, first Western Mountain, second Defile Mountain, third Dog Mountain, or in poetry "Lovers Leap." Defile Mountain inclines considerably to the north, and is called Beach Hill; between it and the margin land of Dog Mountain, lies Deming's Pond. The road between S. W. Harbor and Somesville lies along with it; some tourist named it Echo Lake, from the constant echoing of every sound that happens on the road. The eastern countenance of Dog Mountain is remarkably grand. It descends, almost perpendicular, all of 900 feet to the surface of Somes' Sound, and then

down ten or fifteen fathoms. In front of Dog Mountain, and back of
Fernald's Point, is Carrol Mountain, which is a perfect minature of
Green Mountain. It is the most picturesque of mountain scenery on
the island. On Dog Mountain, is the famous "Gold Diggins," where
one or two men were led by spirits to uncover the ledge, and watch for
the opening of the granite safes, where Kid and some others burried
their treasures. This fact the author received from the proprietor,
who, generously told him "all about it," and who politely invited him
to inspect the curious, tangible marks which are very prominent.

The eastern shore of the Sound is walled by the slopes of Brown's
or Hadlock Mountain, which is also called Pond Mountain, from the
two ponds on the east. Then, Robbey Mountain, Jordan's Mountain,
Bubble Mountain, Green Mountain, Kebo Mountain, and Newport
Mountain. The huge nameless pile, on the south, is always seen, but
seldom visited. The mountains all slope away gradually to the north-
ward and west-ward, and strike out boldly and perpendicularly on the
east and south. The other mountains, fall but a little short of the
hight of Green Mountain, and blending their grandeur, or throwing
their shadows from one to the other, they lift their caps together, and
all appear at once.

"The island is cleft in the middle" by Somes' Sound, a deep, swift
bay or lake nearly five miles long. It took its name from Abraham
Somes, the first settler who maintained his position on Mt. Desert. It
is narrow and bold, even to the verge of the mountains on either
shore, and widens and shoals at the source and mouth. There are
four fresh water lakes or ponds; three lying north and south across
the line between Tremont and Mt. Desert—all west of Somes Sound.
First, Seal Cove Pond or "Lily Lake," as some one named it for the
many pond lilies that grow in it,—Great Pond and Deming's Pond, or
"Echo Lake." In Eden, between Jordan's and Green Mountains, is
Eagle Lake, or Pond. There are, of course, many smaller ponds, too
many to notice. Looking from the top of either mountain, the low-
land seems pierced by holes, just like a lot of springs. The island is
surrounded by bays, except on the north where it is separated from
the mainland by Jordan's River,—on the east, Frenchman's Bay,
south, Placentia Bay, west, Bluehill Bay and Morgan's Bay, and just
out side of these is the ocean. The topography consists of mountains,
hills, and plains, ponds, lakes, rivers and bays, all on the verge of the
Atlantic Ocean.

SCENERY.

"Never need an American look beyond his own country for the sublime and beautiful of natural scenery."—*Irving.*
"Mt. Desert is a little world of itself."—*W. W. A. Heath.*

The island has been "written up" so many times, and by so many classes, that it seems weakness for one reared on its fountain soil, to attempt a description. No less a poet than Whittier—has pictured it with his pen, while others, local and foreign, have lent their talents to its wonderful impression. Artists have painted its most striking features, and tourists have sketched all over it. Reporters have interviewed it, and writers have described it, all in their most eloquent and vivid styles, but not once has it been magnified or over-represented, —it is *multum in parvo*—its bronzed statuary and wavy tile-land, when the moon strikes deep into the night, fairly imitates the "torso of Hercules" in great shadows and spreads, obicular, the embellished walls of Pantheon. The

> "Mysterious round! what skill, what force divine,
> Deep felt, in these appear! a simple train;
> Yet so delightful mixed, such kind art,
> Such beauty and beneficence combined;
> Shade, unperceived—so softening into shade;
> And all so forming an harmonious whole.—"

There is not a hill-top or cross road on the whole Island void of something picturesque—but facts alone will here be given, and the reader must imagine or see the rest. The points of greatest interest are on the eastern side of the Island,—the ragged cliffs—the Gorge—the "Spouting Horn"—the "Devil's Oven" and the "Schooner Head," where

> "Ye headlong torrents, rapid and profound;
> Ye softer floods, that leap the humid maze
> Along the road; and thou, majestic main,
> A secret world of wonders in thy self."—

The eastern scenery is wild and awfully grand, and the western, placid and sublime, like nature in her milder mood.

"The Gorge" is the valley between Mt. Kebo and Newport Mountain. The road from Bar Harbor down round the sea-shore runs through it. "Schooner Head" took its name from the likeness of a fore-and-aft schooner—its two masts, sails all set, and bow-sprit with headsails. On this headland is the cleft in solid rock, the "Spouting Horn." It resembles, in form, "The snow-bank tunnel," as though some one had commenced on the shore and shoveled into the bank a distance, and then taken a turn up and out through the top. The water flows in smoothly when calm, but during a heavy south-east wind it rushes in with such force as to dash the spray, with deafening roar, up through the Horn many feet above the tops of the trees into the air. The "Devil's Oven" is a little to the south of the Horn. It is a huge cave worked out of the softer rock, by the architect, "Storm King." Its seething and groaning is fearful, when the billows chase their leader in among the anemones and sea hay.

Over on the western side of the Island, the scenes are very different,—smooth bays and coves—a better chance for boating. "Morgan's Bay" and "Patten's Bay" are always smooth and beautiful in the strongest winds, and island and bay scenery far exceeds that of any other point. The "Look Out" on Bartlett's Island, where the U. S. Coast Survey have a station, one mile from "Lily Lake" is very fine—superior to that of the western gaze from Green Mountain. The tourists miss a great deal unless they drive on the road from Somesville to Centre Harbor, by the "Mill on the Floss," and round the upper end of the three lakes.

De Tocqueville describes the evening thus:

"The traveller holds his breath to catch the faintest sound of life. You hear a church-bell, or a woodman's axe, or the report of a gun, or the barking of a dog, or, at any rate, the indistinct hum of civilized life. Now all is motionless, all is silent beneath the leafy arch. It seems for a moment as if the Creator had withdrawn His countenance, and all nature had become paralyzed."

"A charming scene of nature is displayed."

GLACIAL PHENOMENA ON MT. DESERT.

A contribution of Professor Louis Agassiz, to the Atlantic Monthly, is here quoted for the benefit of those who have so much wondered over the curious marks, and scratches of the ledges, queer grooves, odd impressions, and foreign looking rocks. It is an able production on the glacial philosphy, and those who read it are delighted and confirmed.

"The picturesque island of Mt. Desert is separated from the mainland by a narrow arm of the sea. Much higher in the centre than on the margin, its mountains seem, as one draws near, to rise abruptly from the sea. It is cleft through the middle by a deep fiord, known as Somes' Sound, dividing the southern half of the island into two unequal portions; and its shores are indented by countless bays and coves, which add greatly to its beauty. We entered the island by the northwestern side, from Trenton, and proceeded at once to Bar Harbor, on the eastern side, a favorite resort in summer on account of its broken, varied shore, and of the neighborhood of Green Mountain, with its exquisite lake, sunk in a cup like depression half way up the mountain side, and its magnificent view from the summit. At the very entrance to the island, on passing over the toll bridge at Trenton, there is an excellent locality for glacial tracks. The striæ are admirably well preserved on some ledges at the Mt. Desert end of the bridge. The trend of these marks is north-northeast, instead of due north as in most localities; and here is one of the instances where this slight deflection of the lines is evidently due to the lay of the land. The island is not only highest towards the centre, but narrows at the northern end as it sinks down toward the shore, from which it is separated on either side by two deep fiords running up into the coast of Maine, and known as Frenchman's Bay on the east, and Union Bay on the west. It is evident that the mass of ice passing from the mainland over this arm of the sea sunk eastward and westward into these two gorges, acquiring, no doubt, additional thickness thereby, and, in consequence of this change in its normal course, was slightly deflected from its usual direction in working its way up against the shores of Mt. Desert. This is shown by the fact that glacial marks on the northwest shore bear as I have already said, slightly to the east, while those on the northeast shore bear slightly to the west. On approaching the centre of the island the marks converge towards each other, and regain their primitive direction due north and south, on its more elevated position. The morning following my arrival at Bar Harbor I spent in examin-

ing the glacial phenomena in its immediate neighborhood. At Bar
Harbor itself, the marks bear north and north-west. A mile further
south they are all in a north-north-westerly direction. The cove of the
Spouting Horn, however,—a deep recess in the rock, where the surf
acts with wonderful force,—is engraved on both sides with lines running due north. On the same side of the island, considerably to the
south of Bar Harbor, there is a striking sea-wall composed of coarse
materials, thrown up in a line along the shore, formed, no doubt, by
some unusually severe storm, coinciding with high-water. It resembles the well known sea-wall of Chelsea Beach. Behind this wall
stretches an extensive marsh, formerly a part of the sea. Somewhat
beyond it, on the shore, are two very distinct and polished grooved
surfaces, with the lines running due north. On the afternoon of the
same day, I ascended Green Mountain. Along the lower part of the
road the marks run north-west, then north-north-west, converging
more and more toward normal course, until, after passing the first
summit, and thence upward, they lose entirely the slanting direction
impressed upon them by the deflection of the ice about Frenchman's
Bay, and run due north again. All the way up the last slope of the
mountain, wherever the rock is exposed, may be seen well-engraved
flat surfaces of rose-colored protogyne on which the scratches and
and grooves sometimes run for twenty feet without any perceptible
interruption. On the very summit is a quartz dike cut to the same
level with the general outline of the knoll, on which the marks are
very distinct. I arrived on the extreme point where the southern descent is so abrupt that the mountain seems to plunge into ocean, just
at sunset. The sea, as far as the eye could reach, was still glowing
with color; amethyst clouds floated over the numerous islands to the
south-west; while on the other side in the gathering shadows lay the
little lake midway on the mountain slope, and, below, the many inlets,
coves, and islands of Frenchman's Bay.

On the following day, we crossed to the opposite side of the island,
skirting Somes' Sound, and the next morning entered the Sound in a
small schooner. A stiff breeze from the north, which obliged us to
tack constantly, and made our progress very slow, prevented us from
exploring this singular inlet for its whole length; but short as it was,
our sail gave me ample opportunity for observing the glacial phenomena along its shores. At the mouth of the Sound before entering the
narrows, there are several concentric terminal moraines on both sides
of the fiords. No doubt they once stretched across it, and have been
broken through by the sea. On either side, to the right and left, in
ascending the Sound, are little valleys running down to the water; and
evidently they have all had their local glaciers, for there are terminal
moraines at the mouth of each one. These facts only confirmed my
anticipations. I had seen, on passing the head of the fiord, in our
drive of the previous day, that it must, from its formation afford an
admirable locality for glacial remains, unless they had been swept
away by the sea. The town of Somesville is beautifully situated at
the head of Somes' Sound. Approaching it from the east, I observed
that the glacial marks which had been pointing due north began to
point west-north-west, while on the western side of the settlement they
pointed east-north-east. Evidently there is an action here similar to
that by which the marks are deflected on the northern side of the
island about Frenchman's Bay and Union Bay. The mass of ice coming from the north had been gradually sinking into the fiord from
opposite sides. Near Somesville church the marks run due north
again.

The extensive surface of polished and scratched rock in this locality recall the celebrated Helle-Platten of the valley of Hasli. From South West Harbor we followed the shore to Bass Harbor and Seal Cove. There are frequent indications of glacial action along this road, and one or two points of special interest. At Bass Harbor there is a large dike of green trap running at right angles with the tide current. Though regularly overflowed at high-water, the action of the sea has not affected the glacial characters, which are so peculiarly distinct at this spot. Not only is the dike itself deeply scored with striæ and furrows running due north, but being of a softer quality than the granitic rock which it intersects, it has been cut to a little lower level, and the vertical walls of the fissure are polished, scratched and grooved in the same way. I met here with one of the instances showing the character of the working-class in America which always strike a European with astonishment. There was a blacksmith's shop near by, and being extremely anxious to obtain a specimen from it on account of the clearness of its glacial characters, I requested the head workman, who had been looking on with considerable interest, to break me off a piece. It was not an easy task, for there were no angles, the dike being sunk below the surrounding surface and perfectly smooth. After a time, and not without considerable hard work, a wedge was driven in, and with the help of a crow-bar two or three very satisfactory specimens were pried out. I naturally wished to pay the man for his labor; but he refused to take anything, saying that I was a geologist travelling for the sake of investigation. He added, that he subscribed for one or two papers and magazines; perhaps he should meet with some of the published results of the journey one of these days, and that would be the best reward for the little help he had given. Seeing his interest in the object of my researches, I explained to him the significance of this dike, showing to him the marks pointing straight to the north, and evidently entirely independent of tidal action, since they ran at right angles with it. As I bade him good bye, he said, ' Henceforth this dike shall be my compass; I shall know when the wind blows due north.' The locality was, indeed, especially interesting from several points of view. It is one of the few instances I have seen in which a dike, being composed of a softer pate than the adjoining rock, has yielded more readily to the ice-plow, and is cut to a lower level, thus forming a broad, flat furrow, the upright wall of which is scored as deeply as the horizontal surface of the dike.

At Seal Cove, however, on the south-western shore, the marks have again a north-westerly direction. South of Seal Cove all the surface inequalities are *Moutonées*, the striæ running north-north-west. We returned to Trenton bridge by the western shore, having skirted the whole island.

The coast range east and west of Somes' Sound is divided into a series of hills by transverse valleys, in most of which are small lakes formed by transverse moraines at their southern extremity. Beginning east, and not counting the less prominent peaks, we have, first, Newport Mountain; next, Kebo and Green Mountains; then, Jordan Mountain, Robbey Mountain, Hadlock or Pond Mountain, and Westcot Mountain, all to the east of Somes' Sound; then following Dog Mountain, Defile Mountain, Beach Hill, and West Mountain, all on the west side Somes' Sound; Denning Pond, which I have examined more at detail, lies between Dog and Defile Mountains. The road along the lake follows the eastern or left or lateral moraine of glacier which once filled its basin; and the lake itself is hemmed in by a crescent-shaped terminal moraine at its southern extremity.

The lakes, eleven in number, intervening between the other moraines are likewise bordered by moraines. We have thus satisfactory evidence that at an early period of the retreat of the great ice-field covering this continent, when it no longer moved over the highest summits of the land, local glaciers were left in the gorges facing the sea.

Mount Desert itself must have been a miniature Spitzbergen, and colossal icebergs floated off from Somes' Sound into the Atlantic Ocean, as they do now-a-days from Magdalena Bay."

The head-workman mentioned in this chapter, as wedging out a portion of dike, was William N. Abbott of Tremont, who was afterward rewarded by a complimentary pamphlet from the author—Prof. Agassiz—who published the result of his journey in 1867.

RESOURCES OF THE ISLAND.

The resources of the Island are its wood, lumber, granite, and maritime privileges. Farming is quite conspicuous, but the soil is too rocky to make it extensively profitable, though there are many fine farms on the Island, which are carried on quite successfully. The harvest is not plenteous enough to fill every granary, and in the spring many of the farmers or planters have to buy seed. Wild pasture-land is quite abundant, and cattle find their fodder from May until November. Some keep their stock earlier and later, some later and earlier, but these are the average months for turning out and driving up. There is but little hay imported at present, and stock is constantly increasing. There is a dyked marsh of 150 acres at Bass Harbor, Tremont, which yields quite abundantly—far more than any up-land in the best cultivation. The table-land of Eden is more productive than most parts of the Island, probably because it is more dressed. About one-half of the Island has been improved. The wood and lumber cover the remaining portion. There is but little of the forest in its primeval state, it has been cut and culled thoroughly, yet it is well composed of old growth spruce, fir, pine, cedar, birch, maple and hemlock. The woods are inexhaustible for the Island use, but the exports are telling fast upon the growth—one hundred per cent. faster than the growing—faster even than the people are aware—kiln-wood is a regular winter business all over the Island, and the mills are worked to their utmost capacity.

There are two steam saw-mills—one at Pretty Marsh, Mt. Desert, and one at Salisbury's Cove, Eden,—and ten water power saw-mills at different places. The "Hydrographic Survey of Maine," Walter Wells, Superintendent, credits the Island with "Eighteen and more powers." Eden, four powers. First, Hadley's Mills, in the west part of the town; stream fed by a pond. Second, above Higgin's Saw-Mills. Third and fourth, on Eagle Pond stream, two saw mills; stream fed by three or four small ponds. Mt. Desert, four powers, on the Somes' stream; fall 30 feet in 50 rods; power improved by mills which work about ten months in the year. The stream is connected with three powers; the largest five by one and one-half miles; the others, each three and one-fourth by one-half miles. The powers could be increased very considerably, and are, in fact, sufficient for mills of any description, by using the best style of wheels and machinery. Freshets harmless, the water being kept back by dams. An excellent harbor at the place, (Somesville) where vessels load and unload within ten rods of the outlet of the stream. Tremont, ten powers, and more. First and second on Heath's Stream," the outlet of Seal Cove Pond, and emptying into Seal Cove, a convenient and safe harbor. Upon one, a saw-mill; upon the other, a grist-mill. The productions of the mills can be shipped without the expense of trucking. Annual lumber productions about 250,000 M.; several hundred thousand staves. Total fall, 40 feet in one-fourth of a mile; two dams; mills work about three-fourths of a year, but with proper improvements could run the whole year; stream connected with two ponds. Third, fourth, &c., on Heath's Stream, never improved; carry by flumes. Sixth, &c., at Bass Harbor, shingle mill; six months in the year. The stream is five miles long; fall 60 feet in the whole distance. Seventh, eighth, &c., on large brooks, with sufficient power to manufacture small lumber. Ninth, tenth, &c., tide privileges, none of which are improved. Bass Harbor, Duck Cove, and Norwood's Cove.

The granite which has lately been tried, and now being worked, is pronounced of the first quality, by the quarrymen; and the quantity immense. A quarry has just been opened on the west side of Somes' Sound.

The maritime coast of Mt. Desert is, of all other resources, the most improved. The safe harbors and convenient departure make it valuable to shipping. The fishing and coasting is the principal business, which is proved by the fact that land is more valuable round the sea-shore, especially at those points where tourists and rusticators make their head-quarters, at the hotels and summer boarding-houses. The settlements are along the shore principally, and where the best accommodations for fishing, and convenient coasting are, there the growth and increase are the fastest. Every harbor is occupied and interested in shipping, building and sailing. The vessels owned are all commanded and manned by natives, and many a fine foreign and American ship is sailed by an Islander. Every year, some new vessels "leap into the ocean's arms," and going out, compete successfully with other ports. The coast is well lighted, and the lights well tended and seldom does an Islander mistake his reckoning and go ashore.

MODERN HISTORY AND REMINISCENCES.

The "Modern History" of Mt. Desert dates back to the spring of 1761, when Captain Abraham Somes of Gloucester, Mass., took up a land grant as a part of that commonwealth, came to the head of the lake now known as Somes' Sound, built a mill on the stream and place where the "Somes Mill" now stands, and made other improvements. Capt. Somes had visited the place before, in some of his voyages; he was pilot on the New England coast and even beyond either way; being the man who piloted the first English Navy Fleet into Halifax, N. S., he understood perfectly the resource of Mt. Desert. He did not move his family down to the place which bears his name, and where he built a house, until later in the year, when Mr. James Richardson and family joined them, and made their habitations together. Mr. Richardson was a man of education and refinement, and quite popular in local history. He chose for his work, lumbering in winter and farming in summer. He was of the Scotch-Irish descent, and Capt. Somes of the English. In a year or two others were induced to make their home on the Island, among them Stephen Richardson, brother to James, who located himself at Bass Harbor. Soon the islands round began to be settled. Bartlett's Island, by Christopher Bartlett, who got a deed of one hundred acres from the General Court of Massachusetts, for which he paid five dollars, or its equivalent, just what it cost to make the deed and survey the land. Israel Bartlett, brother to Christopher, took up a grant and settled himself at Pretty Marsh at the time his brother went into the island which bears his name.

Eden became settled in 1763, by a family named Thomas. The Cranberry Isles became settled about the same time. Bancroft's History, relating to Mt. Desert, says:—"The native Indians were the Canibas, and Algonquins of the Abewaki nations.

RESOLUTION INCORPORATING PLANTATIONS IN THE PROVINCE OF MASSACHUSETTS.

In the House of Representatives, February ye 15, 1776.

Resolved, That the plantations within this colony not incorporated, and they are hereby impowered to call a meeting of the inhabitants; which meeting shall be warned by a Justice of the Peace residing nearest the plantation or place where the meeting is to be held; which Justice shall issue his warrant in proper form to call a meeting to some principal inhabitant of the plantation, directing him to set a copy of his warrant in some public place in said plantation, the hand fourteen days before said meeting; and when the inhabitants of any plantation or place so warned and assembled as aforesaid, they shall have the same privilege of choosing a committee of Correspondence, inspection and safety as if they were incorporated into a town, as provided by this court, per resolve, dated February ye 15, 1776, and their doings shall be valid to all intents and purposes as if they were incorporated into a town.

Sent up for concurrence.

· WILLIAM COOPER, Speaker pro tem.

In Council, February 16, 1776. Read and concurred.

PEREZ MORTON, Deputy Secretary.

Benjamin Greenleaf, Walter Spooner, Michael Farley, Jabez Fisher, Thomas Cushing, John Whitcomb, John Taylor, Benjamin White, Joseph Palmer, Benjamin Lincoln, Elead Taylor, Caleb Cushing, Moses Gill, Jedediah Foster, Samuel Holten.

A true copy, Attest:

PEREZ MORTON, Deputy Secretary.

LINCOLN, SS. *To Mr. Stephen Richardson of the Island of Mt. Desart.*

According to a state resolve of this colony, you are hereby required to warn and notify all the freeholders and inhabitants of the island of Mt. Desart and Cranberry Isle and Plasentia Isle, to assemble and meet at the house of the above named Stephen Richardson on Saturday, the thirteenth day of this instant month March, at ten of the clock before noon, then and there to act upon the following particulars, viz:

1st. To vote and choose a moderator to regulate said meeting.
2d. To vote and choose a Clerk.
3d. To vote and choose three, five, seven or nine persons for a Committee of Correspondence, Safety and Inspection, in such places as they may think most convenient.

4

4th. To vote and act upon any other article or matter which you may think best to agree upon when assembled as above. This to be posted up in some public place within the above mentioned boundary, or a copy thereof fourteen days beforehand and for which, this shall be your warrant.

Given under my hand at my dwelling house at Narragnagus, this twelfth day of March in the sixteenth year of his Majesties reign, A. D. 1776.

ALEXANDER CAMPBELL, Justice of the Peace.

The residence of Stephen Richardson was at that time on what is now called Crockett's point, west side of Bass Harbor, Tremont. The house went out of existance some time ago, but the debris of the cellar still remains.

PLANTATION ORGANIZATION MEETING.

MT. DESART, March ye 30, 1776.

In District meeting assembled according to the foregoing warrant.

1st,   *Voted* Mr. Josiah Black moderator for this meeting.

2d,   *Voted* James Richardson, Clerk.

3d,   *Voted* that there be five men chosen a committee of Correspondence, safety and Inspection for the ensuing year.

4th,   *Voted* Messrs. Ezra Young, Levi Higgins, Stephen Richardson, Isaac Bunker and Thomas Richardson be that Committee.

5th.   *Voted* that Messrs. Ezra Young, John Thomas and Abraham Somes be a committee to bring in the order of the day.

6th,   *Voted* that Messrs. John Tinker, Thomas Wasgatt and Abraham Somes be a committee to take care of the meddows on this and the adjacent islands, both salt and fresh, that strangers may not destroy them or any other privileges belonging to the islands.

7th,   *Voted* a booke be provided for the records of this district by subscription.

8th,   *Voted* James Richardson be Treasurer of this Dist. That the committee call on John Tinker and Amasiah Scalland to render an account of what hay was cut and carried off the island last year. (Five other articles are here recorded which relate to the laying out and building of roads to different parts of the island.

15th.   *Voted* that this meeting stand adjourned until the tenth day of next June, to meet at the house of Stephen Richardson, James Richardson, Clerk.

The adjourned meeting opened at the time and place specified.

Voted to raise and form a company of militia, and elected for officers, Ezra Young, Captain, Abraham Somes, 1st Lieutenant, Livi Higgins, 2d. Lieutenant.

Voted that the committee of Correspondence, Safety and Inspection apply to Major Shaw for the provisions granted by the colony. Adjourned. James Richardson, Clerk.

Another warrant dated March 5, 1777, was issued to Ezra Young by Alex. Campbell, directing him to warn together the freeholders and inhabitants of Mount Desart, Cranberry Isle and little Plasentia Isle, for the purpose of choosing officers and doing plantation business. The meeting was held at Stephen Richardson's house, March 25, 1777, and presided over by Josiah Black. James Richardson, Clerk. Daniel Rodack, Amasiah Leland, Abraham Somes, Benjamin Bowden and Daniel Gott. were elected a Committee of Correspondence, Safety and Inspection, and Plantation Assessors.

All the annual plantation meetings were warned by a Justice of the Peace, the Inhabitants having power to hold adjourned meetings only, without a legal warrant.

At the plantation meetings, a careful and vigorous supervision of town affairs was laid out, regulating all the roads, cutting of the hay, warning suspicious or lazy people out of town, which was most practically applied by the plantation officers.

On the 1st day of June, 1778, the inhabitants of Mt. Desert, Cranberry and Plasentia islands assembled themselves at the house of Stephen Richardson, for the purpose of "giving approbation or disap. probation to a form of government, which, with the three amendments was adopted. At this meeting, "voted to see if we can agree upon some method to encourage the destruction of the varmint that destroys our grain.

In 1780, there being no "Justice" within thirty miles of the island, a couple contracted and formed their own marriage ceremony, which at that time was lawful.

The agreement, as recorded, is here given.

MARRIAGE RECORD OF NICHOLAS THOMAS AND LUCY SOMES.

MT. DESART, February 22d, 1780.

This is to sartify that, inasmuch as there is no Lawful Authority within thirty miles of this place, whereby we can be married as the Law directs—we do, with the consent of our parents, and in presence of these witnesses, solemnly promise and engage to each other in the following words:—

I, Nicholas Thomas. do, in the presence of God, angels and these witnesses, take Lucy Somes to be my married wife to live with her, to love, cherish, nourish and maintain her in prosperity and adversity, in sickness and health, * * * * and to cleave to her alone as my only and lawful wife, as long as God shall continue both our lives.

I, Lucy Somes, do, in presence of God, angels and these witnesses, take Nicholas Thomas to be my married husband, to live with him, to honor and obey him in all things lawful, in prosperity and adversity, in sickness and health, and * * * * to cleave to him alone as my only and married husband as long as God shall continue both our lives.

Signed, { NICHOLAS THOMAS, [L. S.]
{ LUCY SOMES, [L. S.]

In presence of these witnesses :—

Signed,
{
James Richardson,
Samuel Reed,
James Richardson, jr,
Daniel Richardson,
Abraham Somes.

A true copy, attest, Abraham Somes, Clerk.

Persons not a few, are living to-day who can testify to the long, happy and prosperous union of the above parties, and their descendants are as worthy and honorable as any that grace the Island of Mt. Desert.

AN ACT FOR THE CORPORATION OF THE TOWN OF MT. DESART.

Commonwealth of Massachusetts. In the year of our Lord one thousand seven hundred and eighty-nine.

Incorporation of the plantation of Mt. Desart, so-called, in the County of Lincoln, into a town by the name of Mt. Desart.

Be it enacted by the Senate and House of Representatives in General Court assembled, and by the authority of the same, that the plantation called Mt. Desart, together with the islands called Cranberry Island, Bartlett's Island, Robertson's Island and Beach Island, together with the inhabitants thereon, be and they are hereby incorporated into a town by the name of Mt. Desart, and the said town is hereby vested with all the powers, privileges and immunities which other towns in the commonwealth by law do or may enjoy.

And be it further enacted, that Gabriel Johonnot, Esq., be and hereby is impowered to issue his warrant, directed at some principal inhabitant of said town, requiring him to notify the inhabitants thereof to meet at such a time and place as he shall therein appoint; to choose all such officers as towns by law are required to choose at their annual meetings.

In the House of Representatives, February 16, 1789.
This bill having had three several readings, passed to be enacted.
WILLIAM HEATH, Speaker pro tem.

In Senate, Febuary 17, 1789.
This bill having had two several readings, passed to be enacted
SAMUEL PHILLIPS, President.

Approved.

JOHN HANCOCK, Governor,

A true copy, attest.
JOHN AVERY, Jun'r Secretary,

ORGANIZATION OF THE TOWN.

A warrant dated Penobscot, April 6, 1789, by Gabriel Johonnot, Esq., to Abraham Somes, called the inhabitants together at the house of Abraham Somes.

The oath of allegiance was presented and signed by over one hundred persons. The officers elected were, Ezra Young, Moderater; James Richardson, Clerk; Levi Higgins, Abraham Somes, Stephen Richardson, Thomas Richardson, and Ezra Young, Selectmen.

John Hancock received thirty votes for Governor.

Samuel Adams received twenty-three votes for Lieut. Governor.

Daniel Coney received twenty-two votes for Senator.

Adjourned to the fifteenth day of June.

The records by James Richardson present a very fair though faded appearance, uniform in matter, and plain in autography.

FIRST REPRESENTATIVE TO GENERAL COURT.

"MT. DESART, October ye 8, 1776.

Voted, that Stephen Richardson go to the General Court with a partition in behalf of the inhabitants of this Island."

Mr. Richardson's bill was 4 pounds, 22 shilling, which was paid by the plantation—for serving the partition which James Richardson and Ezra Young were paid 12 shilling for making.

One record says:—"The records of the last meeting are in the hands of Mr. Smith, down on Sutton's Island."

In 1828, the General Court of Maine passed a bill entitled, "An act to regulate the Fishery of Alewives in the town of Mt. Desert."

The population of the Island in 1820 was 2.111 persons, and in 1830 it was 2,560, Cranberry Isles 257, which, had it not been set off from the town of Mt. Desert, would have made 2,818.

BATTLE OF NORWOOD'S COVE.

This action occurred on the 9th of August, 1814, commencing Tuesday morning at sunrise, and lasting thirty minutes.

The approach of a ship was seen by Johnathan Rich and his son John, who were fishing in a small boat outside of Duck Island a day or two before the engagement, and as she neared them one of the crew, probably the commander, hailed: -- "Come along side."
" Heave to, and I will," answered the boat. After getting alongside,

the executive officer explained that it was the King's ship, Tenedos, bound in for water, and asked Mr. Rich to stand pilot, who, like a loyal American, refused, although a great price was offered; they traded the fish, though, and while the talk was going on, the youth John, who was afterwards in the battle, was making himself busy counting the guns on a side, and considering the meaning of the figures, "18 pounds," stamped on their muzzles.

The sloop-of-war Tenedos found her way in by sounding, and anchored in the channel between Sutton's and Bear Islands.

At the same two coasting vessels were hauled up at the head of Norwood's Cove, one, "Four Sisters," belonging to Benjamin Spurling, of Cranberry Island; and it is supposed that an enemy of Mr. Spurling, reported this fact to the commander of the English ship, who considered it his prerogative if not his duty, to seize and bond the vessel; acting on this principle an officer was sent ashore to Mr. Spurling's, demanding $350 on this vessel.

Mr. Spurling asked for a little time to raise the money, which was granted, but, instead of doing so, he sent his five sons, Robert, Thomas, William, Enoch and Samuel to raise the militia, and at night informed the officer that the bond could not be met. Two barges were then got ready, the larger containing sixty men and mounting a twelve pound swivel; in this one Mr. Spurling was compelled to go. The smaller one contained forty men and a six-pounder. About twenty-five men under the command of Capt. William Thom of Mt. Desert, lay in ambush on what is now called Clarke's Point. As the larger barge advanced into the cove, Robert Spurling hailed from the shore, warning the English to keep off, but got an insulting answer. "I would fire into you if my father was not there," said Robert. "Oh, never mind me! fire away! fire away!" said the old man, as his white scattering locks polished in the red rays of the coming sun.

The Americans opened fire in true Continental style, coolly and effectively, making the enemy realize the spirit of freedom which dwelt in the hearts of the fisherman and pioneer, on the coast and in the forest, on the land and on the sea, at Mt. Desert as at Boston, ready and active.

The English returned fire hastily and at random; after losing seven men killed and a dozen or more wounded, they very humbly withdrew, leaving the field to the militia.

Samuel Hadlock was wounded in the right forefinger as he fired from behind a tree, being the only American touched; the tree was afterwards cut down and seventeen "king's arm" balls taken out.

A few hours afterwards Benjamin Spurling was released, and the British ship-of-war weighed anchor and went on her way, but probably not rejoicing.

The military organization in 1814 was:—Colonel Black of Ellsworth,

General Commander,—the Mt. Desert company of militia officered by William Thom. Capt., John Lear, 1st Lieut.

Eden company, John O. Hotchkiss, Capt.

An independent company, with Daniel Pepper, Capt.; Samuel Hadlook, Lieut.; William Heath, Ensign.

The relics of the battle are very few; Mrs. Catherine Heath of Seal Cove, (Tremont) has a six-pound cannon ball which her husband, William Heath, Ensign of the Independent Company, picked up just after the battle; some other shot were preserved at the time, but the people considered the action quite insignificant, and they were soon forgotten or wasted.

There are quite a number of persons living who were there—at Norwood's Cove—and they seem to remember, pretty well, what occurred, but their dates are so conflicting that it is necessary to go to the calendar of 1814, by which, the year began on Saturday, and August on Monday—the first Tuesday was the second day of the month, and the second Tuesday was the ninth; they all agree that it was on Tuesday, and somewhat past the first of the month. Now, if any of the veterans are confounded with this statement, (as probably many will read it), let them take the figures, as has been done in this case, and compare with the year.

Insignificant as this may seem or be, the principle contended for was as great as the most brilliant achievement of the war, and the love of liberty swelled the hearts of these humble patriots as fervently as it pulsed the minds of the "great men." All day the minute men, enrolled or not, took their way by paths or boat, to the vicinity of Norwood's Cove and South West Harbor, either in company, squad, or alone, caring only to "defend themselves and their liberties," and prove themselves true to their first principle—American Independence. Young men who fought there, have lived to maintain their sentiments, and again renew their pledge to their country, by sending sons and grandsons to "do what they could" toward crushing the rebellion of the South, some of whom enriched with their bodies, and moistened with their blood the battle fields, and as the earth closed over their shattered frames, the old father caught back the changing spirit and held it out, a dying reproach to the faltering neighborhood.

TOWN OF MT. DESERT.

The Town of Mt. Desert covers about forty square miles, exclusive
of Bartlett's Island, which contains about 1800 acres. The population
in 1970 was 918. The amount of school money raised is $978. There
are twelve school districts—one on Bartlett's Island. The principal
business is lumbering, ship-building and farming. The valuation of
the town in 1871 was $118,884. Wood and lumber is manufactured
quite extensively. Ship building is carried on vigorously at Somesville; the yard of A. J. Whiting & Co. is in almost constant use, and
that of George Somes nearly every year. The Woollen Factory of L.
H. Somes, on the Somes' Stream, does considerable business. The
people at Pretty Marsh farm and lumber,—at North East Harbor farm
and fish. The village at the head of the Sound is the nucleus, active
and honest—busy and fair.

TOWN OF EDEN.

The Town of Eden took its name from the beauties of scenery among
the forests in their primeval state. It was first settled in 1763. The
" act of incorporation " by the General Court of Massachusetts is dated
February 22d, A. D., 1796. The warrant for the first town meeting,
which was held at Salisbury's Cove, was served by Paul Dudley
Jones. (The book which contains the first records has been taken
from the Clerk's Office, and we could not, as in other towns, quote the
early proceedings.) The population of the town in 1870 was 1197.
The valuation of the town in 1871 was $175,500. The amount of
school money raised (1871) $1,250, with the interest on school fund
which amounts to about $100—total $1,350. Number of school dis-
15,—annual average attendance of scholars, 390. It covers about forty-eight square miles,—farming and lumbering principal business.
Greatest scenery in the eastern part of the town. Hotels at Bar Harbor. and steamboat communications and depot.

TOWN OF TREMONT.

STATE OF MAINE. In the year of our Lord, one thousand eight hundred and forty-eight.

" An act to incorporate the town of Mansel. Be it enacted by the Senate and House of Representatives in Legislature assembled, as follows :—

Section 1. All that part of the town of Mt. Desert in the County of Hancock, lying south of a line commencing at Andrew Fernald's north line on Somes' Sound; thence, across the mountain to the head of Deming's Pond; thence, continuing the same course to Great Pond; thence across said pond to the south-east corner of lot number 114, on a plan of said town by John S. Dodge, thence, westerly on the south line of said lot 114, to Seal Cove Pond, and continuing the same course to the middle of said Pond; thence northerly up the middle of Upper Seal Cove Pond to the head thereof, and continuing the same course to the south line of lot marked " Reuben Noble," on said plan ; thence westerly on the south line of said last named lot, to the sea shore, together with Moose Island, Gott's Island and Langley's Island, with the inhabitants thereon, is hereby set off from said town of Mt. Desert, and incorporated into a separate town by the name of Mansel, and vested with all the powers, and privileges and immunities, and subject to all the duties and liabilities of other incorporated towns, agreeable to the constitution and laws of this State, and is classed in the same Representative District as its inhabitants now are.

Section 2. Said town of Mansel shall be holden to pay the said town of Mt. Desert, such a proportion of the debts and liabilities of the said town of Mt. Desert, beyond their resources now existing, and which may hereafter arise in consequence of any and all suits at law now pending in favour or against said town of Mt. Desert; and also to assume the support of such proportion of all persons supported as permanent or occasional paupers of said town of Mt. Desert, as the last valuation of that portion hereby set off, bears to the whole valuation of the town of Mt. Desert.

*	*	*	*	*	*	*	*	*	*	*

Section 6. Any Justice of the Peace within said County of Hancock, may issue his warrant to any legal voter residing in the town of Mansel, directing him to notify the inhabitants thereof, to meet at a time and place specified in said warrant, for the choice of town officers and to transact such other business as other towns are authorized to do at their annual town meetings.

Section 7. This act shall take effect and be in force from and after its approval by the Governor.

In the House of Representatives, June 3, 1848.
This bill having had three several readings, passed to be enacted.
(Signed,)   H. B. McLELLAN, Speaker.

In the Senate, June 3, 1848.
This bill having had two several readings, passed to be enacted.
(Signed,)   CALEB R. AYER, President.

June 5, 1848. Approved.
(Signed,)   JOHN W. DANA, Governor.

Secretary's Office, Augusta, Me., June 5, 1848.
I hereby certify that the foregoing is a true copy of the original deposited in this office.
(Signed.)   JOHN G. SAWYER,
Deputy Sec'y of State.

Tremont, Dec. 4, 1848.
I hereby certify that the foregoing is a true copy from the original certificate of said John G. Sawyer.
(Signed,)   JOHN S. DODGE,
Town Clerk of Tremont.

The sections omitted above, three, four and five, are of minor importance, and would weary more than interest the reader.

A warrant for the first town meeting was issued August 2, 1848, by Wilson Guptill, a "Justice of the Peace" for Hancock County, to John Rich, a legal voter of the town of Mansel, to notify and warn the inhabitants of said town to meet on Wednesday, the 9th day of August, at ten o'clock in the forenoon, at the red school-house in Bass Harbor, to choose all necessary town officers, adjust matters with Mt. Desert, and transact such other business as might legally come before the meeting.

Pursuant to the warrant, Mr. Rich posted a notice at B. Benson, Jr.'s store, (Bass Harbor,) seven days before the meeting.

At the time and place specified, the inhabitants met and were called to order by John Rich. Alfred Harper chosen Moderator, John S. Dodge, Town Clerk; Shubal D. Norton, Seth H. Clark, John S. Dodge, Selectmen and Overseers of the poor; Barnard Rummell, Town Treasurer; Rev. C. M. Brown, S. D. Norton, J. L. Martin, S. S. Committee; Eben Fernald, James R. Freeman, Edwin Kittredge, Jeremiah Moore, Joshua Eaton, Zebediah Rich, Elias Rich, Ambrose Thurston, Wills Carver, Isaac M. Ober, Benj. Norwood, Samuel O. Harper, School Agents; Enoch Lurvey, Andrew Tarr, Horace Durgan, John Dolliver, Joshua Eaton, Robert Rich, John M. Gott, John Murphy, Benj. Atherton, Jr., Benj. Norwood, Samuel O. Harper, Highway Surveyors; Wilson Guptill, David Hopkins, Eaton Clark, James Reed, Joseph Gott, Constables; John Rich, Collector of Taxes;

John F. Norwood, John Rich, James Reed, Joseph Gott, Benj. Gilley, Fence Viewers; William Heath, Eaton Clark, David Hopkins, Pound Keepers; Benj. Benson, Jr., Henry Clark, Abraham Richardson, Auditors of Accounts.

Voted, That the annual town meeting be held on the first Monday in March.

The usual amount of business which naturally occurs at such times was transacted.

The name—Mansel, is the French for Mt. Desert, or Mt. Mansel, as given by Governor Winthrop. It was first adopted as the name of this town in the incorporation act, but it did not wholly suit the townfolks so, on a petition of C. M. Brown and his associates it was changed, by the same Legislature, to Tremont—the last name signifying, in latin, three mountains, which are in the limits of the town, namely, Western Mountain, Defile Mountain, and Dog Mountain.

The population of Tremont in the last census was 1822 persons—as given by William N. Abbott, the census taker. The area is about forty-two square miles, or nearly one-third of the whole Island. The valuation of the town in 1871 was nearly half a million dollars. The number of polls was four hundred and twenty-six. There are fourteen school districts, (two graded—one at South West Harbor, Freeman District, and one at West Bass Harbor,) with an annual attendance of four hundred and fifty scholars. The amount of school money raised in 1871 was about $1875.

CRANBERRY ISLES.

"Gems of the waters!—with each hue
Of brightness set in ocean blue.
Each bears aloft its tufts of trees
Touched by the pencil of the frost,
And, with the motion of each breeze,
A moment seen,—a moment lost,—
Changing and blent, confused and tossed,
The brighter with the darker crossed,
Their thousand tints of beauty glow
Down in the restless waves below,
And trembling in the sunny skies,
As if, from waving bough to bough,
Flitted the birds of Paradise."— *Whittier*.

The Cranberry Isles are best seen from the summit of Green Mountain. There they lie like huge piles of sea-weed floating on the ocean. With its harbors and road-steads, filled with vessels, it is picturesque indeed,—around the south shore the waves heave up—way up—fall over backwards and run down into the sea again,—gather strength, rush on to the assault backed by the "Ocean King of old."

On the north shore the waters gracefully flow to the beach, and pass on their current way. To the south all is confusion and turmoil—to the north, harmony and peace.

These islands are connected in history with Mt. Desert, though not especially spoken of until John Robertson settled on one of them, which is known as Robertson's Island. Williamson's history tells us, " the inhabitants suffered much during the war of the revolution, both from the enemy and for necessaries." It must have been so, when the British occupied Castine, and persecuted all the Americans eastward, yet, to their cause, true as life, they chose every year a committee of correspondence, safety and inspection, which faithfully discharged every duty, working, not solely for the gain of these islands that gemmed the bay, but for the achievement of liberty for the whole continent, and the bettering of their social relations.

The third volume of the Massachusetts Historical Collection of 1764, says :—" After the British troops had taken possession of Penobscot in 1775, it was expected all the country eastward of it would have submitted to their jurisdiction; yet, notwithstanding their proclamation, denouncing vengeance in case of refusal, the inhabitants of Machias, with most of the towns westward still adhered to their country's cause, and continued on the offensive to the close of the war." (The Cranberry Isles are so near related to Mt. Desert Isle, that in speaking of one, Historically, we mean both.)

The militia was under the general command and influence of General Campbell, who placed Colonel Allen of Machias, in command of the friendly Indians.

The inhabitants of Cranberry Isles were always on the *qui vive*, and every approaching sail was vigilantly watched to see if the enemy were coming, as they often did to pillage, and forage, and threaten, and when one did sail in, the news was quickly dispatched to the opposite shore and spread over the Island, to warn people to be on their guard, and drive back into the forests their stock.

The settlement of the Island began the same year with Mt. Desert, at Somesville, by Abraham Somes.

The "Act of Incorporation" bears date of March 16th, 1830. It was incorporated by the General Court of Maine, and embraces Great and Little Cranberry Isles, Suttons Isle, Bakers Isle, and Bear Isle. The population of the town in the last census was 351 persons. The area of the whole town is 1440 acres:—Great Cranberry, 850, Little Cranberry 350, Suttons 200, Bakers 90, Bear 50. There is a meadow or heath on the Great Island which measures 200 acres and is unoccupied save by frogs and rushes. The cost of drainage would be enormous, if, indeed, it could be drained at all, as it is on the level of the ocean. There are five school districts in town, two on the Great Isle, and one on the Little Isle, and one on Suttons Isle, and one on Bakers Isle. The valuation of the town assessed in 1871 was 65,000 dollars; lost during the year by shipping seven thousand dollars, of which, W. P. & W. H. Preble lost nearly four thousand dollars. The general business of the Islands is fishing, there are somewhere about fifteen smoking houses for curing herring—and they contain from 8,000 to 800 boxes each—the herring are taken round the shores by net, and are a little larger than those taken by wier, and not so large as the Magdalen herring.

We present the general appearance of the Islands as they appeared to us on a recent visit there. Landing on the shore of the Great Isle, at Preble's wharf, we first saw the stand of fish—houses— flakes and barrels—ready to receive the deep sea fish— cod, hake and haddock, the smoke house and box shed, tubs and fishing gear. Then, up through a large pretty field, to the Preble House. This Hotel is neatly finished, and elegantly furnished, and ornaments the Island. A road, from the upper to the lower end of the island, built along by pretty cottage houses, and an approach of gardens, laid round with even fields and farmed patches. Down to the pool, which is formed by a hook like point of land, boats and fish-houses appeared again.

Holden & Richardson are doing business at the pool. They have a store well stocked, with such goods and wares as are usually found in a country sea-port store,—outfits for the fishermen—they maintain a smoke-house, buy and cure all kinds of fish.

On the Little Isle, which lies a mile East of the Great Isle, is the fish yard of W. E. & G. Hadlock. They send their own vessels to the banks, and such other places as will further their business, buy and cure with their own, those of the boat fishermen, which employs quite a lot of men. Their "business" is the largest of the kind carried on "Down among the Islands."

Suttons, Bear, and Bakers Isles form a part of the same business as the Great and Little Isles. There are two light-houses—one on Baker's Isle and one on Bear Isle, which guide into a safe harbor, or along the coast.

> "Lonely coast-light set
> Within its wave-washed minaret."

In leaving the Cranberry Isles, we here tender our thanks to W. H. Preble for the assistance he so ably rendered, and to the Preble House for its kindness.

The first town or organization meeting, was called by a warrant issued by Aaron Wasgatt, Esq., Justice of the Peace, on application of Enoch Spurling and als., and held on the Great Island.

The first election made :—

SAMUEL HADLOCK, }
ENOCH SPURLING, } Selectmen.
JOSEPH MOORE, }

ENOCH SPURLING, Clerk.

GOTT'S ISLAND.

In 1789, the General Court of the commonwealth of Massachusetts, empowered a committee of three persons, consisting of Samuel Phillips, Jr., John Reed, and Leonard Jaro, to sell the land in the counties of Cumberland, York, and Lincoln, not already appropriated.

Daniel Gott of Mt. Desert, obtained a deed from this committee, dated March 25th, 1879 which conveyed to him for and in consideration of the sum of eighteen pounds legal money, two small islands described as little Plasentia Island, measuring 222 3-4 acres, and Bar Island, measuring 83 1-4 acres, situated in the Lincoln County. The deed was acknowledged before Samuel Cooper, Justice of the Peace, and recorded in the Lincoln County Registry of deeds, August 7th, 1789, Lib. 23, Vol. 246, by A. W. T. Rice, Register.

Mr. Gott occupied until his death, July 7th, 1814 the larger mentioned island, from which, the name it now bears was derived.

The Island is now occupied by ten families, comprising a school district of Tremont,—affording convenience for fishing, wiering and farming, which is most thoroughly and vigorously improved.

Prior to 1789, Little Plasentia was transiently occupied, but no homestead made.

In 1742 it was inhabited by Indians, and an incident of that date may amuse some who will follow these lines :—

Some parties belonging in Boston had bought land with water privileges at Machias, and had lumber mills in operation, with a quantity of men employed there. A small coaster was kept plying between these two ports, conveying lumber, and supplying the employees with provisions. On one of her down trips, the vessel, well laden with "all such," run ashore on a shoal of the bar, which makes between the Island and Bass Harbor, at half ebb tide. The deck of the vessel was soon crowded with dusky neighbors ; the chief taking command said : " Ugh, all one Injun vessel now ! "

" Yes, said the captain, all one Injun rum, too."

" Ugh, rum ! " said the chief ; " me have much rum ashore."

The crew set about lively getting a barrel of " fire water " ashore for the feathered, top-knotted jaw-jaws, and in a little while the whole tribe were leaping and yelling in the wildest manner round the "festive board " a green corn dance.

At mid-night, quite another scene painted the island, for "silence reigned profound." At the coming of the tide, the vessel floated, while a stirring land breeze fanned her out to sea. Sometime in the morning the chief awoke, and after surveying his charge exclaimed:— "All gone vessel! all gone rum! Indian he no good!"

GENERAL REMARKS.

The schools of Mt. Desert rank above the average of common schools, and the school houses are the best in the county; the school house at East Bass Harbor is the largest of the kind in the county, —there are more new than old ones on the Island, indeed, there are but one or two real old ones, and they will very soon give way to new ones,—many of the houses have halls in the upper story, some of which are used by the graded schools. The Island furnishes its own —regular trained--teachers—mostly, and some are called to teach in larger or higher schools in other places. The annual average attendance to all the schools on the Island is more than one thousand, and enough money is carried away by students to other schools to form and support one of the highest order on the Island, and still maintain their reputation as teachers.

In reviewing the work before us, we see many discrepancies, valleys and hills. The ancient history we have condensed from Williamson, De Costa, Henne and Bancroft,—the modern history and reminiscences from local records and tradition,—the *business* we have gathered by the assistance of different persons and believe it to be nearly perfect. The topography is from the work of H. F. Walling,—the scenery is from personal observations, and is submitted, with the whole, for such corrections as more able resources may develop, or present mistakes demand.

To show the gain of the Island in ten years, we give the census of 1860 here:—

Cranberry Isle,	347, gain	4
Eden,	1246, loss	49
Mt. Desert,	916, gain	2
Tremont,	1768, gain	54
Total gain, 11.		

The valuation of the towns has increased at a good interest—in Mt. Desert and Tremont by shipping and fishing, and in Eden by building and improved farming.

Some of the inhabitants still cling to the opinion that money lies buried over the Island somewhere, especially along the shore, and that diligent search might unfold it,—that the mountains are immense treasure houses of gold and silver,—that the fields are a covering to slate and marble beds,—that the forests hide gold mines, and that granite is as abundant as the earth itself, " if they only knew it."

That Mt. Desert is to be a great " watering-place and resort," no one doubts,—every summer brings new comers, and none leave without a desire to re-visit. The hotels filled every year, faster even than they build, but the private residences are always open to accommodate. Bar Harbor and South West Harbor are at present the most conspicuous places, but it is probable, that when the roads are completed to the top of the other mountains, the company will flow that way.

The firms advertising in this book are selected, and are all first class. Some will need no references as their reputation has placed them beyond inquiry. The people on the Island are generous and hospitable, and of the true yankee blood "ready for a trade."

The religious are Evangelical and Christian, and the churches well supported. The Island has been well represented abroad; among its moral standard bearers was the late Bishop Davis Wasgatt Clark.

> " An island, full of hills and dells,
> All rumpled and uneven
> With green recesses, sudden swells,
> And odorous valleys driven
> So deep and straight, that always there
> The wind is cradled to soft air."—*Browning.*

Tinker's Island, which belongs to Tremont, is a "gem of the bay " with green roads arched over by big birch trees. A visitor is always welcome at Capt. Tinkers.   Truly &c.,   AUTHOR.

TREMONT, July 1871.

Insurance Agents.

Names.	Residence.	P. O. Address.
Roscoe G. Salisbury,	Somesville,	Mt. Desert.
John Somes,	"	"

Artists.

Benj. F. Wade,	Somesville,	Mt. Desert.

Blacksmiths.

E. C. Parker,	Somesville,	Mt. Desert.
Elisha Wasgatt,	"	"
Geo. W. Haynes,	Bartletts Isle,	"
Wm. Callihan,	Long Pond,	N. E. Harbor.

Boot & Shoe Makers.

John Conners,	Somesville,	Mt. Desert.
Lewis Somes,	"	"
Lewis Somes, Jr.,	"	"
Benj. D. Baker,	Beach Hill,	"

Carpenters, & House Builders.

John H. Parker,	Somesville,	Mt. Desert.
S. P. Richardson,	"	"
H. S. Seavey.	"	"
B. T. Atherton.	"	"
George S. Parker,	"	"
Joseph Southard,	N. E. Harbor,	N. E. Harbor.

Churches.

Names.	Residence.	P. O. Address.
Union Church,	Somesville,	Mt. Desert.

Civil Engineers & Surveyors.

J. D. Parker,	Somesville,	Mt. Desert.

Clergymen.

E. R. Osgood,	Somesville,	Mt. Desert.

Cloth Dressers & Finishers.

Lyman H. Somes,	Somesville,	Mt. Desert.

Country Stores.

A. J. Whiting & Co.,	Somesville,	Mt. Desert.
J. Hamor & Co.,	``	``
Nash Brothers,	``	``
Green G. Stevens,	``	``
L. J. Higgins.	``	``
Daniel Kimball,	N. E. Harbor,	N. E. Harbor.
Stephen Southard,	Long Pond,	``
Charles Raymond,	Bartletts Isle,	Mt. Desert.

Dress Makers.

Kate Stevens,	Somesville,	Mt. Desert.
Adelma F. Somes,	``	``
Cynthia H. Smith,	``	``
C. Moore,	``	``
Lucretia S. Bartlett,	Bartletts Isle,	Mt. Desert.

Woolen Factories.

L. H. Somes,	Somesville,	Mt. Desert.

Herring Fish Curers.

E. E. Babson.	Somesville,	Mt. Desert.
Geo. B. Somes,	``	``
R. L. Somes,	``	``
Giles H. Sargent.	``	``
Samuel Gilpatrick.	N. E. Harbor,	N. E. Harbor.
Thomas Manchester,	``	``
Sans Whitmore.	``	``
Thomas A. Wasgatt,	``	``
J. & H. Bartlett,	Bartletts Isle,	Mt. Desert.
F. Salsbury.	``	``
Decatur Dawes,	Pretty Marsh.	``

Halls.

Names.	Residence.	P. O. Address.
Hamors Hall,	Somesville,	Mt. Desert.
Masonic Hall,	''	''

Hotels.

Mt. Desert House, D. Somes,	Somesville,	Mt. Desert.

Justices of the Peace.

Daniel Somes,	Somesville,	Mt. Desert.
J. D. Parker,	''	''
B. T. Atherton,	''	''
John H. Parker,	''	''
Daniel Kimball,	N. E. Harbor,	N. E. Harbor.

Lumber Dealers.

John Somes,	Somesville,	Mt. Desert.
John W. Somes,	''	''
John J. Somes,	''	''
Thaddeus S. Somes,	''	''
A. J. Whiting,	''	''
Daniel Somes,	''	''
George B. Somes,	''	''
R. L. Somes,	''	''
Cousins, Higgins & Co.,	Town Hill,	West Eden.

Stone Masons.

Isaac Hutchinson,	Somesville,	Mt. Desert.

Mills.

Grist & Saw Mill,	Somesville,	Mt. Desert.
Shingle & Box Mill,	Cross Road,	''
Steam Mill,	Great Pond,	''
Saw Mill,	Head Sound,	''

Milliners.

Kate Stevens,	Somesville,	Mt. Desert.
A. F. Somes,	''	''

Music Teachers.

F. Grindle,	Somesville,	Mt. Desert.

Notary Public.

J. D. Parker,	Somesville,	Mt. Desert.

Physicians.

Robert L. Grindle,	Somesville,	Mt. Desert.
Rufus Grindle,	''	''

Post Offices.

Names.	Residence.	P. O. Address.
1st, Office,	Somesville.	Mt. Desert.
2d, "	N. E. Harbor,	N. E. Harbor.

Post Masters.

Jonathan Hamor,	Somesville,	Mt. Desert.
B. F. Roberts,	N. E. Harbor,	N. E. Harbor.

Ship Builders.

John W. Somes,	Somesville,	Mt. Desert.
T. S. Somes,	"	"
J. J. Somes,	"	"
A. J. Whiting,	"	"

Ship Carpenters.

Wm. P. Smith,	Somesville,	Mt. Desert.
Benj. F. Leland,	"	"
Wm. Reed,	Oak Hill,	"
Hugh Richardson,	"	"
H. A. Keniston,	Pretty Marsh,	"

Ship Joiners.

John H. Parker,	Somesville,	Mt. Desert.
H. S. Seavey,	"	"
S. P. Richardson,	"	"
Joseph Southard,	Long Pond,	N. E. Harbor.

Telegraph Office,

in A. J. Whitings Store,
Operator R. G. Salsbury, Somesville, Mt. Desert.

Tinsmiths.

M. D. Stevins, Somesville, Mt. Desert.

Wool Carders.

L. H. Somes, Somesville, Mt. Desert.

EDEN BUSINESS DIRECTORY.

Insurance Agents.

Names.	Residence.	P. O. Address.
Leonard J. Thomas,	Eden,	Eden.

Blacksmiths.

Daniel W. Brewer,	Hull's Cove,	Salis'y's Cove.
Albert F. Higgins,	Bar Harbor,	East Eden.
Samuel H. Richards,	Eden.	Eden.
John S. Salisbury,	Bar Harbor,	East Eden,
Oliver P. Thomas,	Eden,	Eden.

Boat Builders.

Simeon H. Richards,	Eden,	Eden.

Boot & Shoe Makers.

John Wasgatt,	Eden.	Eden.
Daniel Ladd,	West Eden,	West Eden.

Calkers & Gravers.

George Rinalda,	Salisbury's Cove,	Salis'y's Cove.

Carpenters & House Builders.

Samuel N. Emery,	Salisbury's Cove,	Salis'y's Cove.
Hosic R. Hamor,	" "	" "

Carpenters & House Builders, (Continued.)

Names.	Residence.	P. O. Address.
Lewis Higgins,	Bar Harbor,	East Eden.
Bancroft W. Thomas,	Eden,	Eden.
George W. Richards,	"	"
Albert Hadley,	West Eden,	West Eden.
John S. Lyman,	East Eden,	East Eden.

Churches.

Baptist Church,	Eden,	Eden.

Coopers.

Frederick Wilcomb,	Salisbury's Cove,	Salis'y's Cove.
Henry Wilcomb,	Eden.	Eden.
Edward Young,	Salisbury's Cove,	Salis'y's Cove.

Country Stores.

Eben W. Hamor,	West Eden,	West Eden.
B. C. Thomas,	Eden,	Eden.
L. J. Thomas,	"	"
Peleg Young,	Salisbury's Cove,	Salis'y's Cove.
Joseph W. Wood,	"	"
T. L. Roberts,	East Eden,	East Eden.
Edward Desisle,	Bar Harbor,	" "
R. Kittredge,	" "	" "

Halls.

Youngs Hall,	Salisbury's Cove.
Sewing Circle Hall,	West Eden.

Hotels.

Mountain House,
Carpenter & Brewer, Prop'rs, Summit Green Mt.,   Eden.
Agamont House,
Tobias Roberts, Proprietor,   Bar Harbor,   East Eden.
Atlantic House,
J. H. Douglas, Proprietor,   " "   " "
Bay View House,
Hamor & Co., Proprietors,   " "   " "
Deering House,
Chas. Higgins, Proprietor,   " "   " "
Eden House,
Ash Brothers, Proprietors,   " "   " "
Hamor House,
James Hamor, Proprietor,   " "   " "
Harbor House,
A. F. Higgins, Proprietor,   " "   " "
Kebo House,
A. J. Mills, Proprietor,   " "   " "

Hotels, (Continued.)

Names.	Residence.	P. O. Address.
Newport House,		
M. L. Roberts, Proprietor,	Bar Harbor,	East Eden.
Rockaway House,		
T. L. Roberts,	" "	" "
Rodick House,		
D. Rodick, Proprietor,	" "	" "
St. Sauveur House.		
Fred A. Alley, Proprietor,	" "	" "
Way Side Inn,		
R. G. Higgins, Proprietor,	" "	" "
Ocean House,		
Samuel Higgins, Proprietor,	" "	" "

Justices of the Peace.

L. J. Thomas,	Eden.	Eden.
E. M. Hamor,	West Eden,	West Eden.

Meeting Houses.

Western House,	Eden.	Eden.
Eastern House,	East Eden,	"

Builders & Ship Carpenters.

Seth Harding,	West Eden,	West Eden.
Emmons Pray,	" "	" "
J. H. Mayo,	" "	" "
Alex Higgins,	" "	" "
Atwater Higgins,	" "	" "
Alfred Mayo,	" "	" "
J. Richardson,	Eden.	Eden.
J. Salisbury,	Bar Harbor.	East Eden.
Uriah Goodridge,	Salisbury's Cove,	Salis'y's Cove.
Fred Leland,	" "	" "
W. Leland,	Eden.	Eden.
Otis Brewer,	Hulls Cove,	Salis'y's Cove.

Masons & Plasterers.

David Leland,	Eden,	Eden.
Otis Leland,	"	"

Mills.

J. B. Hadley's,	Eden,	Eden.
Higgins & Emery's,	"	"
Page & Co.'s,	Salisbury's Cove,	Salisb'y's Cove.

Post Offices.

Eden,	Eden,	Eden.
West Eden,	West Eden,	West Eden.
Salisbury's Cove,	Salisbury's Cove,	Salis'y's Cove.
East Eden,	Bar Harbor,	East Eden.

Post Masters.

Names.	Residence.	P. O. Address.
L. J. Thomas,	Eden,	Eden.
Wm. T. Thomas.	West Eden.	West Eden.
Uriah Goodridge,	Salisbury's Cove,	Salis'y's Cove.
T. L. Roberts.	Bar Harbor,	East Eden.

Surveyors of Wood, Lumber & Bark.

Eben M. Hamor,	West Eden,	West Eden.
Alex Higgins,	" "	" "

Telegraph Office,

Telegraph Operator,		
Miss S. B. Reynolds,	Bar Harbor,	East Eden.

Teachers.

Gideon Mayo,	West Eden,	West Eden.
Edgar W. Higgins.	" "	" "
Bloomfield Higgins,	" "	" "
Alonzo Higgins,	Eden,	Eden.
Sidelia Mayo,	West Eden,	West Eden.
Judith Thomas,	" "	" "
Lizzie Wasgatt,	Bar Harbor,	East Eden.

7

TREMONT BUSINESS DIRECTORY.

Insurance Agents.

Names.	Residence.	P. O. Address.
Abraham Richardson,	Bass Harbor,	Tremont.
E. H. Dodge,	" "	"
H. H. Clark,	S. W. Harbor,	S. W. Harbor.

Nursery Agent.

James Clark,	Goose Cove,	Tremont.

Steamboat Agent.

Henry Clark,	S. W. Harbor,	S. W. Harbor.

Express Agent.

H. H. Clark,	S. W. Harbor,	S. W. Harbor.

Sewing Machine Agent.

Thomas Clark,	Goose Cove,	Tremont.

Auctioneer.

Benj. Benson,	Bass Harbor,	Tremont.

Blacksmiths.

J. R. Freeman,	S. W. Harbor,	S. W. Harbor.
W. H. Rae,	" "	" "
Benj. Robbins,	Centre,	Seal Cove.
Anam Ober,	"	" "
John O. Rich,	Bass Harbor,	Tremont.
Frank Young,	Goose Cove,	Tremont.
John Young,	" "	"
George Kellay,	Cross Road.	Seal Cove.

Boarding Houses.

Names.	Residence.	P. O. Address.
A. K. P. Lunt's	Goose Cove,	Tremont.
David Clark,	Centre,	Seal Cove.

Boat Builders.

Eaton Clark,	Bass Harbor,	Tremont.
Amos B. Newman,	" "	"
Wm. Gilley,	S. W. Harbor,	S. W. Harbor.
Benj. Newman,	" "	" "
Wm. Clinkard,	Centre,	Seal Cove.

Boot & Shoe Makers.

Robert Ash,	S. W. Harbor,	S. W. Harbor.
Wm. Lawler,	Norwoods Cove,	" "
J. G. Wilson,	Bass Harbor,	Tremont.

Bowling Alley.

S. H. Clark's,	S. W. Harbor,	S. W. Harbor.

Calkers & Gravers.

James Newbury,	Bass Harbor,	Tremont.
Preston A. Rich,	" "	"
J. G. Wilson,	" "	"
Wm. Herrick,	S. W. Harbor,	S. W. Harbor.
Wm. H. Clinkard,	Centre,	Seal Cove.
Matthew Sewart,	Cape District,	" "
Ira Reed,	" "	" "
James Kellay,	Goose Cove,	Tremont.

Carpenters & House Joiners.

James A. Peckham,	Bass Harbor	Tremont,
Jacob Sawyer,	" "	"
James L. Wilson,	" "	"
Wilson Guptil,	" "	"
Levi Lurvey,	S. W. Harbor,	S. W. Harbor.
Sans Stanley,	" "	" "
John D. Lurvey,	" "	" "
Samuel Lurvey,	Norwoods Cove,	" "
J. T. Clark,	Goose Cove,	Tremont.
Wm. A. Clark,	" "	"
Reuben Murphy,	" "	Seal Cove.
David Clark,	Centre,	" "
Jonathan Norwood,	Cross Road,	Seal Cove.
Joseph M. Kellay,	Goose Cove,	" "
N. B. Kellay,	" "	" "
Josiah Swett,	Seal Cove,	" "

Churches.

Names.	Residence.	P. O. Address.
Congregational,	Tremont,	Tremont,
Methodist,	"	"
Baptist,	"	"
H. C. Association,	"	"

Civil Engineers & Surveyors.

Levi B. Wyman,	Seal Cove,	Seal Cove.
W. W. A. Heath,	" "	" "

Clergymen.

J. A. L. Rich, Methodist,	Norwoods Cove,	S. W. Harbor.

Coopers.

Myrtle Johnson,	Bass Harbor,	Tremont.
Reuben F. Keene,	S. W. Harbor,	S. W. Harbor.

Country Stores.

S. A. Holden, & Co.,	Bass Harbor,	Tremont.
C. M. Holden, & Co.,	" "	"
O. M. Kittredge,	" "	"
Benj. Benson,	" "	"
Daniel Gough,	" "	"
Thomas Clark,	Goose Cove,	"
A. Lopaus,	" "	"
James Flye,	Seal Cove,	Seal Cove.
S. H. Robbins,	Centre,	" "
Reuben F. Keene,	S. W. Harbor,	S. W. Harbor.
H. J. Anderson,	" "	" "
J. W. Freeman,	" "	" "
Clark & Parker,	" "	" "

Deputy Sheriff.

Jacob Sawyer,	Bass Harbor,	Tremont.

U. S. Deputy Collector.

D. P. Marceys,	S. W. Harbor,	S. W. Harbor.

Express Office.

Eastern Office,	S. W. Harbor,	

Cod Fish Curers.

David King,	S. W. Harbor,	S. W. Harbor.
W. H. Ward.	" "	" "

Herring.

Names.	Residence.	P. O. Address.
S. H. Clark,	S. W. Harbor,	S. W. Harbor.
H. H. Clark,	" "	" "
Clark &. Parker,	" "	" "
Eaton Clark,	Bass Harbor,	Tremont.
S. A. Holden,	" "	"
Rae, Baldwin, & Rich,	Gotts Island,	"
Reed & Atherton,	Moose Island,	"
T. C. Dow,	Cape District,	Seal Cove.

Factories.

Lobster Factory,	S. W. Harbor,	
Wm. Underwood, & Co.,	67 Broad St.	Boston Mass.

Halls.

Union Hall,	E. Bass Harbor,	Tremont.
——— Hall,	S. W. Harbor,	"
Lopaus Hall,	Goose Cove,	"

Hotels.

Island House,		
H. H. Clark, Proprietor,	S. W. Harbor,	S. W. Harbor.
Freeman House.		
J. R. Freeman, Proprietor,	" "	" "
Ocean House,		
N. Teague, Proprietor,	" "	" "

U. S. Inspector.

S. A. Holden,	Bass Harbor,	Tremont.

Justices of the Peace.

L. B. Wyman,	Seal Cove,	Seal Cove.
W. W. A. Heath,	" "	" "
Benj. Sawyer,	" "	" "
A. Richardson,	Bass Harbor,	Tremont.
C. M. Holden,	" "	" "
Wilson Guptil,	" "	" "
H. H. Clark,	S. W. Harbor,	S. W. Harbor.
D. P. Marceys,	" "	" "

Circulating Library.

West Bass Harbor,	Bass Harbor,	Tremont.

Meeting Houses.

Union House,	S. W. Harbor.	
" "	Centre.	

Masons & Plasterers.

Names.	Residence.	P. O. Address.
John M. Gott,	Goose Cove,	Tremont.
A. T. Gott,	" "	" "
David Gott,	" "	" "
James Ober,	Centre,	Seal Cove.
Aram Ober,	"	" "

Stone Masons.

Reuben Billings,	S. W. Harbor,	S. W. Harbor.
Seth H. Higgins,	" "	" "
Frank Young,	Goose Cove,	Tremont,

Saw and Grist Mills.

W. W. A. Heath,	Seal Cove,	Seal Cove.

Shingle & Lath.

Eaton Clark.	Cross Road,	Tremont.

Millmen.

E. P. Dodge,	Seal Cove.	Seal Cove.
W. E. Clark.	Bass Harbor,	Tremont.

Milliners.

Ella M. Kittredge,	Bass Harbor.	Tremont.
H. M. Gott.	" "	"
Hannah Gilley.	S. W. Harbor,	S. W. Harbor.

Painters.

Nathan Stanley.	Norwoods Cove,	S. W. Harbor.
T. E. O. Dodge.	"	"
Walter Stanley.	"	"

Physicians.

Wm. A. Spear,	Bass Harbor,	Tremont.

Post Offices.

Bass Harbor.		
Eaton Clark, P. M.	Bass Harbor,	Tremont.
Seal Cove,		
James Flye, P. M.	Seal Cove,	Seal Cove.
S. W. Harbor,		
J. T. R. Freeman, P. M.	S. W. Harbor,	S. W. Harbor.

Rigger.

James Tinker.	Goose Cove.	Tremont.

Sail Maker.

Albert Bartlett.	S. W. Harbor,	S. W. Harbor

Ship Carpenters---Masters.

Names.	Residence.	P. O. Address.
Henry E. Newman,	S. W. Harbor,	S. W. Harbor.
Wm. S. Newman,	" "	" "
Samuel Newman,	" "	" "

Ship Contractors.

C. M. Holden, & Co.,	Bass Harbor,	Tremont.
S. A. Holden, & Co.,	" "	"
A. Richardson,	" "	"
Hiram Flye,	Seal Cove.	Seal Cove.
H. H. Clark,	S. W. Harbor,	S. W. Harbor.
A. Haynes,	" "	" "

Ship Carpenters.

Daniel Eaton,	Bass Harbor,	Tremont.
W. P. Sawyer,	" "	"
A. B. Newman,	" "	"
J. F. Norwood,	" "	"
Eaton Clark,	" "	"
M. P. Rich,	Duck Cove,	"
Elias Rich,	" "	"
J. R. Rich,	" "	"
Jonathan Rich,	" "	"
Joseph M. Gott,	Goose Cove,	"
Otis W. Morey,	Seal Cove,	Seal Cove.
Benj. Sawyer,	" "	" "
John Moore,	S. W. Harbor,	S. W. Harbor.

Ship Joiners.

James L. Wilson,	Bass Harbor,	Tremont.
J. A. Peckham,	" "	"
J. T. Clark,	Goose Cove.	'.
Sans Stanley,	S. W. Harbor,	S. W. Harbor.

Traders.

Isaac Gott,	Bass Harbor,	Tremont.
James Powers,	Seal Cove,	Seal Cove.

Telegraph Offices.

Miss A. M. Holden, Operator,	Island House,	S. W. Harbor.
Miss Victoria Marceys, "	S. W. Harbor,	" "

Turner.

Josiah Swett,	Seal Cove,	Seal Cove.

CRANBERRY ISLE BUSINESS DIRECTORY.

Insurance Agents.

Names.	Residence.	P. O. Address.
Wm. P. & Wm. H. Preble,	Great Island,	Cran. Isle.
A. C. Fernald,	Sutton's Island,	" "

Auctioneer.

Wm. P. & Wm. H. Preble,	Great Island,	Cran. Isle.

Blacksmiths.

Henry Fernald,	Great Island,	Cran. Isle.

Boarding House & Hotel.

Preble House,		
Wm. P. Preble, Proprietor,	Great Island,	Cran. Isle.

Boat Builders.

Enoch Spurling,	Great Island,	Cran. Isle.
E. B. Stanley,	" "	" "

Carpenters & Joiners.

Edward Brewer,	Great Island,	Cran. Isle.
Henry Fernald,	" "	" "
Enoch Spurling,	" "	" "
Amos Howard,	" "	" "
E. B. Richardson,	Sutton's Island,	" "

Church.

Names.	Residence.	P. O. Address.
Union,	Great Island,	Cran. Isle.

Coffin Manufacturers.

A. C. Fernald,	Sutton's Island,	Cran. Isle.

Coopers.

Moor & Fernald,	Sutton's Island,	Cran. Isle.

Deputy Sheriffs.

Wm. P. Preble,	Great Island,	Cran. Isle.
B. H. Spurling,	" "	" "

Fish Curers and Dealers. Oil.

W. E. & G. Hadlock,	Little Island,	Cran. Isle.
Wm. P. & W. H. Preble,	Great Island,	" "

Hall.

Hadlocks Hall.

W. E. & G. Hadlock, Prop'r,	Little Island,	Cran. Isle.

Fish Inspector.

A. C. Fernald,	Sutton's Island,	Cran. Isle.

Master Ship Builder.

E. R. Richardson,	Sutton's Isle,	Cran. Isle.

Merchants.

Holden & Richardson,	Great Island,	Cran. Isle.
W. P. & W. H. Preble,	" "	" "
W. E. & G. Hadlock,	Little Island,	" "

Music Teacher.

Miss Fannie A. Preble,	Great Island,	Cran. Isle.

Notary Public.

W. P. Preble.	Great Island,	Cran. Isle.
A. C. Fernald,	Sutton's Island,	" "

Post Office & Post Master.

Joseph S. Spurling,	Great Island,	Cran. Isle.

Sail Maker.

James A Morris,	Little Island,	Cran. Isle.

8

Surveyors of Wood, Lumber & Bark.

W. P. Preble,	Great Island,	Cran. Isle.
L. H. Bray,	" "	" "
A. C. Fernald,	Sutton's Island,	" "

Justices of the Peace·

W. P. Preble,	Great Island,	Cran. Isle.
W. H. Preble,	" "	" "
G. T. Hadlock,	Little Island,	" "
A. C. Fernald,	Sutton's Island,	" "

www.ingramcontent.com/pod-product-compliance
Lightning Source LLC
Chambersburg PA
CBHW022035080426
42733CB00007B/836